guinea pigs

for beginners

by mervin f. roberts

All photographs by the author unless credited otherwise.

The author is indebted to Mr. and Mrs. Gordon Garvin of Old Lyme, Conn., who made their home, their children, and their pets available for photography; also, Mr. Richard Smith of Groton, Conn., who opened his entire establishment to the camera.

ISBN 0-87666-198-3

Distributed in the U.S. by T.F.H. Publications, Inc., 211 West Sylvania Avenue, PO Box 427, Neptune, NJ 07753; in England by T.F.H. (Gt. Britain) Ltd., 13 Nutley Lane, Reigate, Surrey; in Canada to the book store and library trade by Beaverbooks Ltd., 150 Lesmill Road, Don Mills, Ontario M38 2T5, Canada; in Canada to the pet trade by Rolf C. Hagen Ltd., 3225 Sartelon Street, Montreal 382, Quebec; in Southeast Asia by Y.W. Ong, 9 Lorong 36 Geylang, Singapore 14; in Australia and the South Pacific by Pet Imports Pty. Ltd., P.O. Box 149, Brookvale 2100, N.S.W. Australia; in South Africa by Valid Agencies, P.O. Box 51901, Randburg 2125 South Africa. Published by T.F.H. Publications, Inc., Ltd, the British Crown Colony of Hong Kong.

Teaching your guinea pig to eat from your hand is easy . . . if you begin handling him when he is only a few weeks old. He will feel confident and have no fear of people if he is treated properly and always offered tidbits that he likes. A brown long-hair boar enjoys a nutritious cabbage leaf.

Sunshine and vitamins are important elements for a guinea pig's health and long life. This short-hair enjoys both by having a romp in the yard (supervised closely by his owner) and a fresh carrot.

CONTENTS

INTRODUCTION

When Herbert Hoover was President of the United States, everyone knew that if a guinea pig were lifted by its tail, its eyes would drop out. No one needed a book to tell him that. It was common knowledge then, because in 1930 the guinea pig was having its heyday as a desirable common pet. Today the guinea pig is still desirable, but far less common.

The guinea pig is a one-pound tailless South American rodent. It is an odorless vegetarian, gentle, long-lived, easy to rear, available in many colors, and in many hair lengths and degrees of roughness. It is fairly quiet, inexpensive to feed, resistant to disease, pleasant to handle, and difficult to sell. This book contains details about each of the items listed above, excepting Herbert Hoover.

What does it look like? A healthy, normal guinea pig looks like an eggplant with feet. It is cylindrical, about eight to ten inches long and short-legged. It is somewhat thinner at its head end than at its tailless other end. Its hair may be long or short, smooth or rough. The color can be white, cream, yellow, tan, sepia, brown, grey, black, or mixed. The eyes can be any of several colors. When viewed from above, it is difficult to tell which way a long-hair is facing except when it is eating.

Actually the guinea pig is a cavy, not related in anyway to the pig. Where it got the name "guinea pig" is also confusing, since it does not come from Guinea in Africa, or from the Guianas of South America. Some authorities speculate that the "guinea" derives from an old English word meaning foreign; or possibly cavies were first sold in England for 21 shillings—a guinea. They may have

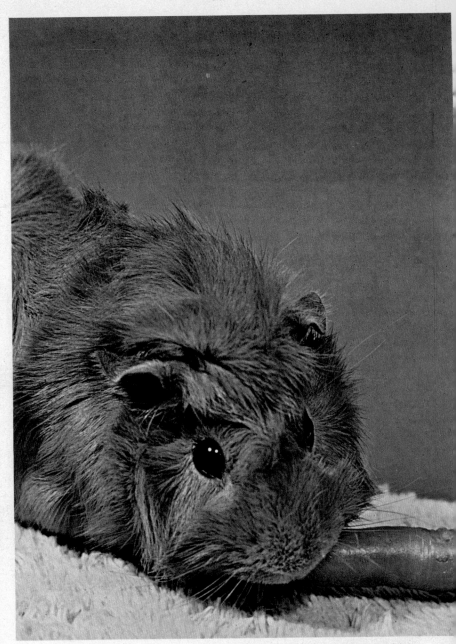

Healthy guinea pigs have bright eyes and a glossy coat and are frisky and alert. Long-hairs require daily brushing and occasional bathing to keep well groomed.

Your pet will love to climb all over you, searching for that inevitable treat. Guinea pigs enjoy occasional freedom, but they must be protected from other pets and neighborhood stray animals. Photo by Louise Van der Meid.

first come to England on slave ships, via Guinea. As to the "pig"—they do squeal, whistle and grunt—all sounds suggesting swine; and their form is squat and rounded. Today, in English, the female is called a sow and the male a boar. Most Americans refer to them as guinea pigs, and most of the British fanciers call them cavies.

Names sometimes used for the same species are restless cavy, Cuy, *Cavia cutleri*, aperea, couie, Abyssinian cavy (a rough-haired variety), English cavy (the normal wild type short-hair), and Peruvian cavy (a long-haired variety).

Other popular rodent pets are usually smaller than a guinea pig. A big old boar might weigh nearly three pounds, but a pet white rat seldom exceeds a half pound, and of course, a hamster weighs about a quarter pound. The only larger pet rodent is the rabbit. Some hares, usually raised in Europe for food, may go up to 15 or 20 pounds, but technically rabbits and hares are not counted as rodents.

This is a matter for taxonomists, not pet keepers to settle; but briefly the difference is in the teeth. In guinea pigs and other rodents, the upper chisel teeth resemble their lower counterparts (*simplicidentata*). In rabbits the upper teeth are paired (*duplicidentata*). Cavies have four toes on their front feet and three on the rear. Sometimes four toes appear on rear feet. This is nothing to get excited about—it is known to scientists; but pet keepers should not use this stock for breeding.

There are several other similar looking rodents less well known and less frequently kept as pets. These include the chinchilla—famous for its fur, but too expensive and delicate for ordinary pet keeping; pacas; agoutis; capybaras; viscachas; pikas and coypus. Some of these are hunted for food or hides or both, but none has all the desirable pet qualities of the cavy.

8

In Peru today, one may obtain live cavies whose ancestors were domesticated by the Incas. Succeeding generations have been in captivity since then—possibly over a thousand years of domestication. Even there, they are available in various colors and hair lengths. The pure undomesticated wild strain is also available through Peruvian hunters, but when it enters the market place it is usually dead, having been trapped or shot for food.

The guinea pig is of the phylum Chordata—it has a spinal chord; of the class Mammalia—it suckles its young; of the order Rodentia—it has chisel-like front teeth; of the suborder Simplicidentata—the upper and lower front teeth resemble each other; of the family Caviidae—it is short-tailed or tailless; of the genus *Cavia*—with four toes on each front foot and three on the rear; of the species *cutleri* or *porcellus*—it depends on which book you read.

After all the trouble of classifying the animal and then wondering about its correct name, it is apparent that science is exact, but not all scientists agree exactly. Some older texts refer to the cavy as *Cavia cutleri*, and more recent texts call it *Cavia porcellus*.

In Peru, where people know a cavy when they see one, it is dressed for the table by slaughtering and scalding in hot water to loosen the hair. Then, the skin is scraped with a knife to remove the hair; it is gutted and finally roasted.

Impress upon the dog that he must not bother the guinea pigs but take no chances. Keep them in a covered cage at all times. Photo by Louise Van der Meid.

A toothbrush is the best implement with which to groom a long-hair. This tan and white long-hair is a show specimen. The American Cavy Breeders Association will send information on local shows if you should decide you want to enter your pet in a show. Photo by Louise Van der Meid.

CHAPTER I.

HABITS

Let's examine the wild ancestors of our domestic guinea pigs and look for hints to guide us in their care. To begin with, they are found in arid, mountainous regions of Peru. There are not many trees, but the ground supports shrubs, bushes, grasses. Rain is infrequent and plants store water in their tubers and roots. Days are warm and sunny; nights are clear, cold and dry. Predators are uncommon, probably the hawk is the guinea pigs' greatest enemy.

Guinea pigs are admirably suited to their environment. They are neither climbers nor swimmers, and have no need to be. They live in colonies to take advantage of each others' burrows and tunnels, and communicate with squeals and grunts and whistles, mostly to warn of danger from enemies. Their voices are not loud, no need to be.

Their coats are not oily, since there is no waterproofing required. They do not bathe or swim or wade. Their claws are simple since they need not climb or even hold their food while eating it. They live in thorny brush and big rabbit ears would get torn—they have small cavy ears instead.

Cavies sleep at night while it is cold. They huddle together in burrows and tunnels for warmth. They are great for families and colonies. They are active during the warm sunny daylight hours. The seasons do not vary much in arid, semi-tropical, mountainous Peru and so there is no need to store food or to hibernate.

Food storage would not be easy for cavies in Peru. They eat tremendous quantities of leafy plants and stems,

This male cavy is happy in a small cage or box. He'll never com-
plain, but he would prefer to have company of his own kind.

rather than smaller quantities of more nutritious foods
like nuts, seeds and grain. This is one important way in
which they differ from the famous hibernating grain
hoarder—the hamster.

Cavies are hardy. They mature slowly: Two months in
the mother's womb; one month to wean; four or five
months more before they should breed. But then they
live seven or eight years, so why rush things?

Even though wild cavies do not have many animal
enemies, they must struggle to exist. This accomplishes
the matter of population control. If every wild female
cavy (commonly called a sow in English) produced twice
the number of young she now produces, the domain
would quickly become overpopulated. The available food
would not suffice and starvation would then limit the

The agouti color is most common among wild guinea pigs, but long hair is usually achieved through selective breeding.

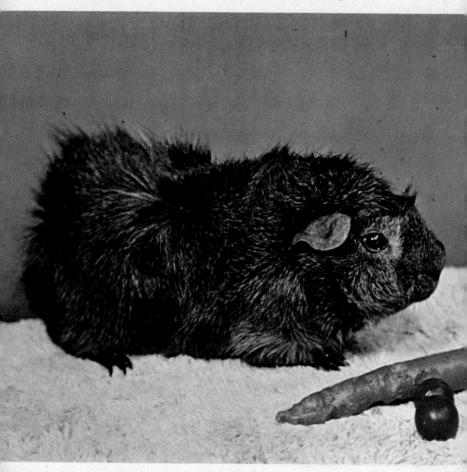

Young guinea pigs are weaned at four weeks and become companionable pets when they are handled by people. The cream long-hair and beige and white short-hair are cagemates and enjoy each other's company as well. Photo by Louise Van der Meid.

population. So wild cavies are not especially prolific. Domesticated cavies are like a horse of another color; man makes a new set of rules and the cavy adapts to them readily.

Cavies do not move violently—no swimming, no running great distances, no climbing—and so it is easy for the sow to carry her young until they are fully developed before birth. Since the wild cavy must go out and forage every day, a large litter of helpless babies to nurse would be an imposition on the sow. The converse is true for the mouse and rat. Also, the mouse, rat and hamster hoard grain, or at least carry it to their nests to eat it.

Cavies occupy a niche in their environment where they specialize to the point of being practically non-competitive with other animals. They eat no insects or other animal life, they occupy no vast tracts to the exclusion of other animals, they do not pollute or monopolize the water supply. Their population is self-limiting without drastic controls like heavy predation, epidemic disease, or migration (like the famous march of the lemmings). All this works to make them ideal pets. They are hardy, long-lived, relatively quiet, clean, inexpensive to feed, easy to rear, gentle—and stupid.

The whistles, squeals and grunts of cavies are mostly for communicating with each other but, stupid as they seem to be, some pets, especially if kept singly · will whistle to their keepers—generally when they hope for some special food. The sounds are cheery sounds, and not considered offensive, but in any case, they cannot be turned off.

In the chapters that follow, the habits mentioned above will be explored in greater detail with emphasis on housing, breeding, feeding, caring for and selling these pets.

CHAPTER II

HOUSING

A dry rocky ground with tunnels through the grass is the clue to housing guinea pigs, or cavies. They like runs, covered nest boxes, privacy in which to sleep, and public areas in which to eat and whistle. Since they do not need climbing surfaces, their cage can be quite shallow or, if deep, it can be provided with perches on top of nest boxes. This two-story arrangement offers more area from the same cube. Ten vertical inches is enough for one level, so a cage 20 inches high might well have a ramp and double deck arrangement to provide nearly twice the floor space for the animals.

One cavy should have a minimum of two square feet in his living quarters, if only to keep his droppings decently away from his food supply. Two cavies in three square feet, and three cavies in four feet would probably be the maximum crowding they could take and still be expected to be healthy, long-lived pets.

The cage size also determines how often their bedding has to be changed. The larger the area per pig, the less frequently it needs to be changed. One guinea pig in six square feet of wood shavings and/or hay could easily go a month without needing his bedding changed. Six animals in the same area would probably begin to smell in two or three days. *You pays your money and you takes your choice.*

Newspaper can be used for bedding. Sheets on the bottom, and shreds to nest in, work nicely. Wood shavings are better still and hay is best. The hay should be fresh (not musty), bright, dry timothy with a little clover in it. Your pet will eat the leaves, seeds and thinner stems,

Cavies are warm-natured animals (their cage temperature should never go below 70 degrees Fahrenheit) and like to snuggle in garments. Their living quarters should provide them with hay and boxes where they can get away from it all occasionally. Tierfreunde Photo

A black-and-white long-haired female with the checkerboard pattern known as tortoiseshell.

An orange-and-white long-haired female of the Abyssinian variety.

An albino has snow white hair and pink eyes. Photos by Louise Van der Meid.

tunnel through the thicker stems and eventually trample down the parts too tough to eat. His coat will become shiny from rubbing against the hay and, although he might possibly scratch his eyes a little on sharp stems, the advantages far outweigh the disadvantages. The eye scratches rarely need medication; in a few days they heal and don't seem to bother the animals. Oat straw is also good bedding, but it has no food value.

Avoid hay which has been sprayed with residual insecticides, since these might prove toxic to the guinea pigs. Whatever bedding you choose, it should be clean, dry and dust free.

The nest boxes need not be elaborate. Wooden or cardboard boxes are fine. One-foot lengths of six- or eight-inch stovepipe may also be used. If there is room, provide several, and the animals will sleep in one, play in another and raise their babies in a third. Leave the tops on the boxes remove only enough of an end to let the animal force its way in. A dark nest box is a happy nest box. The top of the box is not waste space—it becomes a perch.

The cage should be protected from dogs, cats, rats and small children. Cavies are not agile in the sense that cats are agile, and a fall can easily kill or maim them. Keep the cage covered at all times, even if the sides are high enough to prevent escapes.

Wheels and toys are not necessary. The cavy will get his exercise without any expense on your part since generally speaking, cavies are not acrobats like mice, monkeys, squirrels or hamsters.

A large aquarium with a screen cover makes a great guinea pig cage. A twenty-gallon tank makes a good-sized home for one large or two young animals. The furnishings could consist of a thick layer of wood shavings or hay, one or two nest boxes, and a water dispenser or water bowl.

An outdoor hutch with plenty of hay so that the cavies can create tunnels and nests and keep themselves warm at night. This one

Around Florida and the Gulf Coast, cavies can remain out of doors all year long, if the nest boxes are kept full of hay for insulation. The trick here is to stuff the boxes with loose hay so that the animals can create nests secure from chilly night air. Elsewhere in the United States, there are usually at least a few mild months of the year when guinea pigs would benefit from a temporary or permanent outdoor pen; however, they should be brought indoors long before the first frost.

The outdoor arrangement can be a rabbit hutch or dog house with a fence or screened enclosure. Make sure the screen goes all around, and over the top, too. The neighborhood dogs might easily make short shrift of the entire outdoor colony.

Some authors advocate taking these pets out of their cages frequently. When guinea pigs are released on a

Gerbils belong to the rodent family, also. They like toys and exercise wheels, eat fresh vegetables the same as the guinea pig, plus grains and sunflower seeds, but do not get along with each other as well as a colony of guinea pigs does.

The chinchilla, also a rodent, is famous for its fur, expensive, and too delicate to be kept as an ordinary pet. Photo by H. Hansen.

lawn individually, they will scurry for the nearest bush or row of shrubs. If several are released together, they may remain in the open and congregate—especially if there is one bold old boar to act as the leader of the group. Incidentally, two bold old boars is one too many, and you must keep them apart to avoid possible mayhem and bloodshed.

Remember that these pets cannot adjust to wetness or extended periods of intense cold. If you cannot guarantee guinea pigs a dry, warm nest box, don't keep them.

For designs of cages and hutches for cavies, write to the U.S. Department of Agriculture, Superintendent of Documents, Washington, D.C. 20402. Ask for Leaflet 466. They offer inexpensive and authoritative information on small animal cages. If literature on cavies is not available, settle for rabbit information, but make the nest boxes a little lower to give the animals a cozy feeling. Also, bear in mind that the cavy cannot stand the cold or snow that many rabbits thrive in.

If you decide to design your own outdoor hutch, consider something that permits the droppings from the floor to fall through to the ground below. Screen mesh or sticks $\frac{3}{8}''$ apart will work. Also, provide for moving the cage to new grassy areas for fresh forage and to reduce the chance for parasitical infestation. Fleas, worms, flies and ticks will all try to make a living off the pets, but with some little care on your part, the cavies will remain pest free. This is no serious problem if they are provided clean, fresh dry bedding as required.

The cavy is a diurnal animal, it likes daylight, and will bask in the sunlight; but it is necessary to provide some cool shade in the cage in case the sun should get too hot. When setting up the cage, pen or aquarium, remember that the sun swings across the heavens every day and the shadows of 10 a.m. may become the cooking rays of 2 p.m.

CHAPTER III

BREEDING

A guinea pig may be bred when it is only one or two months old, but this is a mistake. The sow is too young to handle the job. Her health is in jeopardy and the offspring are often frail. The resulting small litter—usually only one or two youngsters—isn't worth the rush. Better results are obtained from a female weighing close to two pounds, and fully six months old. The boar should be eight months old before he is used for breeding—again for the same reason. For production purposes, you can expect a useful life of five years from a sow, and a boar might be good for six or seven years.

The litter may be one baby or as many as six. This event can occur as often as five times a year, if the female is bred within a few hours after she gives birth. If she is not bred then, she will not accept a boar until she has weaned her litter—a matter of two or three or even four weeks. Although the young are born fully formed, they should be permitted to nurse for several weeks.

Babies only a day or two old will start to eat semi-solid foods, like bread soaked in milk and some soft vegetables like lettuce and celery. When the young are about four weeks old, they should be examined and separated, according to sex, to keep them from breeding for at least the next four or five months. To determine sex, press the lower abdomen gently while holding the animal in your hands, belly facing you. The sex organ of the male will come out of its sheath.

Here is a short exercise in productivity which should be reviewed before you begin to build cages. Start with some generous assumptions.

Hamsters are much smaller than guinea pigs; they hoard grain and hibernate. They are far more reproductive than guinea pigs, and their lifespan is shorter.

Mice are easy to raise, but the population can explode by thousands per year and as the number of mice increases, so does the odor. They eat all types of grain and seeds.

(1) One litter every two months from every female over four months old.

(2) Average of four young—two males and two females from each litter.

(3) No mortality for the year.

Mate the first pair January 1.

			Totals
Expect 4 young March 1			4
„	„	May 1	4
„	„	July 1	4
„	„	Sept. 1	4
„	„	Nov. 1	4
„	„	Dec. 31	4

Mate the 2 females born March 1 four months later and then in two months expect

Sept. 1		8
Nov. 1		8
Dec. 31		8

Mate the next 2 females born May 1 four months later and then in two months expect

Nov. 1		8
Dec. 31		8

Mate the 2 females born July 1 four months later and then in two months expect

Dec. 31		8

Any animals born after July 1 will not produce that year, so we have from one pair, under ideal conditions, a grand total of 72.

If you are really greedy, you might try to breed the first young females at age two months. By doing this your theoretical maximum output might reach 200 for the year, but your actual maximum output will still probably be 72 or less because of smaller litters and infant mortality.

By comparison with the 200 figure, the mouse can *theoretically* be expected to generate about 1,000,000 offspring in one year; a hamster 100,000 and a rabbit 1,000. In practice none of these figures is obtainable.

Getting back to cavies: From one pair, a pet keeper might expect 20 healthy young in the first year and a professional breeder might be able to squeeze out 50, on the average. For the techniques of breeding, you must use some intelligence and knowledge, but 90 per cent of breeding is simply letting nature take its course.

Now consider the 10 per cent for which you are responsible: You need a mature male and a mature female. A female six months old is at a good starting point. The male might better be eight months old.

You should provide a clean large cage with one or preferably two or even three nest boxes. Plenty of hay is also desirable. All this is to permit the female (sow) to pick the time when she is ready to mate and to keep away from the male (boar) when she is not ready. You might need to provide another cage, in case the sow is abused or roughed-up by the boar. If they do not get along, separate them for a few days and then try again. After things settle down, the pair can remain together for the rest of their lives.

The boar need not be kept out of the nursery so long as there is plenty of room and a place where the sow can hide her young for their first few days. You may discover that she keeps her young in one nest box, she remains in another, and the boar occupies a third spot in the cage. This is perfectly normal. Don't fight it.

With a really large cage or outdoor summer pen with protected nest boxes, you can establish a colony. One old boar (and *only* this one boar) might properly be in command, and as many as eight sows will be happy and pregnant most of the time. You should in every case remove the young boars as soon as they are weaned. Dispose of all but a future replacement for the old boar, if he is over six years old. If one of the young boars is especially

Your local pet shop will have everything you need to keep your guinea pig happy, healthy, and nourished. Photo by Louise Van der Meid.

One of the newer products is a spray shampoo that kills parasites at the same time. Be sure to keep you pet warm and dry him thoroughly after shampooing. Photo by Louise Van der Meid.

desirable for color or hair or some other attribute, you may want to start using him sooner.

Young sows should be isolated from boars until they are at least six months old to permit them to reach maturity before subjecting them to the strain of being bred.

It should be easy to find homes for the extra boars. They are gentle and odorless, excellent pets, and good desktop caged companions for children.

And finally, if (an unlikely "if") your sow produces a litter or two with misshapen or monstrous offspring (i.e., four toes on rear foot, three legs, one eye or misshapen jaw) and she looks normal, don't give up on her until she has been bred to another boar—not related to the boar last used. If her next litter also has a defective baby, do not breed from that sow any more. She can be kept as a pet, of course. If the offspring from the second boar are all sound, possibly the defective gene was inherited by the young from their sire rather than from the dam.

The period of gestation is between 63 to 70 days, and the average time between mating and bearing young is 68 days. The average litter is three, but any number from one to six is normal. A very young or very old sow is more apt to have a smaller litter. Young are born when you least expect them and a normal healthy sow needs no help from you. She will probably cut the cord and eat the sack before you are notified. It is not a good idea to produce young from a sow who has had trouble delivering. You will probably be perpetuating a defect which might better become extinct.

This Abyssinian guinea pig shows the tortoiseshell color pattern. Photo by Eric Jukes.

CHAPTER IV.

GENETICS

The wild guinea pig has black eyes and a brownish-grey coat of short hair. This overall appearance results from the fact that each individual hair is banded with rings of color. When looked at closely, every hair is dull black at the base and then has bands of brown, tan, and/or yellow and finally a shiny black tip. Hair with this pattern is found on many mammals, including woodchucks, rabbits, raccoons and foxes.

This natural wild cavy hair color pattern is called agouti, and is named after the agouti, another rodent of

South America. Agouti is a great protective coloration; and probably those wild cavies which through mutations were born with spots or brighter colors, fell to predators, while the agouti-patterned strain thrived.

In captivity, however, the oddly marked animals are favored, and color varieties have become fixed through selective breeding. This is not difficult to accomplish, even for people who never heard of Gregor Mendel. What animal breeders have done for centuries is simply to mate the animal whose features they liked back to one of its parents or to its brother or offspring, and then mate the offspring with each other (inbreeding) until the desired characteristic prevailed in each generation. This is man's arbitrary selection rather than Darwin's natural selection. In selective breeding, desirability rather than fitness is the criterion.

The eyes of domesticated guinea pigs can be pink, brown or black. The hair can be agouti, black, brown, tan, creamy, orange, yellow, grey, white or mixed. The hair can be smooth or rough—rough is also referred to as whorly. Also, the length of hair can be short or as much as three inches long.

Generally speaking, agouti is dominant over other colors, dark colors are dominant over lighter colors, and shorter hair is dominant over longer hair. No whorls are dominant over whorls and black eyes are dominant over lighter colors of eyes.

Since most textbooks describing guinea pig genetics are written in technical terms, and most guinea pig fanciers eventually begin to wonder what they might expect when breeding their pets, it is about time to introduce a short glossary of genetic terms and then a table of possible offspring from a six-factor back-cross.

In 1928, Professor Sewall Wright of the University of Chicago published a paper in *Genetics*, Volume 13, pages

GLOSSARY

ALLELE—alternative characters. Long hair versus short hair.

BACK-CROSS—the mating of a hybrid to one of its parents.

DOMINANT—a characteristic which results from either a single or double dose of a gene This is contrasted to a recessive which is hidden unless both genes are alike.

GENE—the unit of heredity which controls the development of a character. A character is also called a characteristic, like long hair or pink eyes.

GENOTYPE—the complete genetic makeup of an animal, not necessarily just what shows. The visible aspect is the phenotype. One example could be an agouti short hair. This is a description of a phenotype, but one such individual could be recessive for rough hair or white spots or brown eyes.

HYBRID—the offspring of parents who differ in one or more genes. Also refers to offspring from parents not of the same species. The classic example is the mule, derived from a male donkey (jackass) and a female horse (mare). Hybrids of differing species are usually sterile.

IDENTICAL TWINS—both individuals derived from a single fertilized cell. They are as much alike as the right side of an animal resembles its own left side.

INBREEDING—mating of relatives. Brother-sister, cousins, father-daughter, etc. This will eventually result in establishing a pure breed.

LINKAGE—a tendency for some characteristics always to appear together on an individual. This happens when the genes for these characteristics are all on the same chromosomes.

MUTATION—a sudden genetic change.

PHENOTYPE—the appearance of an individual, as opposed to genotype which is its constitution, not necessarily apparent.

RECESSIVE—a character which shows up only when both of a pair of genes are alike.

VARIATION—the differences within a species. For example, color and hair length among guinea pigs.

508–531. Even today it is a classic. From it the following tables and explanations are derived.

First: Among guinea pigs, these color mutations from the wild type are inherited as recessives.

Dominant	Recessive
SS, No white spots	ss, White spots

(Dominance irregular)

> (S and s are so nicely balanced in their effect that the amount and pattern of the white areas is quite vari-able. Sometimes S behaves as a complete dominant; rather more frequently the hybrid (Ss) has a little white on nose and feet.)

EE, No red spots	ee, Red spots
	(Size and pattern of red spots variable)
AA, Agouti pattern	aa, No agouti bands
CC, Intense color	cc, Red reduced to yellow, black slightly reduced
BB, Black eyes, black hair	bb, Brown eyes, brown hair, red unaffected
PP, Dark eyes, dark hair	pp, Pink eyes, pale sepia or pale brown hair, red un-affected.

This means that the wild agouti pattern comes from the genetic formula—SSEEAACCBBPP.

Second: The pure recessive sseeaaccbbpp is pale brown, yellow spotted, white spotted, without agouti bands, and it has pink eyes. It is not albino. Wright established a colony of this pure recessive variety. Then he crossed them back with their wild ancestors and examined the hybrids. They all looked pretty much like the wild agouti except that a few had small white marks generally on their noses or feet. This you might well expect, since S is not fully dominant over s.

A longhaired guinea pig about to be groomed for showing. Photo by Eric Jukes.

Wright now had the phenotype wild agouti, but the genotype included a recessive for every known color character. These hybrids carried the genetic formula SsEeAaCcBbPp. Since S is not *completely* dominant over s, we will ignore this characteristic for now. For the moment let's consider the five characteristics E, A, C, B, and P. Now, it is a mathematical fact that five pairs of genes will create 32 kinds of eggs and the same 32 kinds of sperms.

What Wright then did was to backcross the hybrid with the pure recessive. He obtained 399 offspring and these were tabulated as visibly distinct types. Now, it so happens that C and c have practically the same effect on black and brown. This caused a lumping of the data in these two categories, but statistical analysis shows that the expected number of about 12 per visible type was obtained.

(SsEeAaCcBbPp) × (sseeaaccbbpp)
(After Wright)

Genotypes	Visibly Distinct Types (eggs and sperms of recessives)	Offspring
e a c b p $\times$		
E A C B P	Black, red agouti	14
E A c B P	Black, yellow agouti	17
E A C b P	Brown, red agouti	11
E A c b P	Brown, yellow agouti	11
E a C B P	Black ⎫	
E a c B P	Black ⎬	28
E a C B P	Brown ⎫	
E a c b P	Brown ⎬	28
e A C B P	Black, red agouti, red spots	12
e A c B P	Black, yellow agouti, yellow spots	13
e A C b P	Brown, red agouti, red spots	10
e A c b P	Brown, yellow agouti, yellow spots	16
e a C B P	Black, red spots	13
e a c B P	Black, yellow spots	7
e a C b P	Brown, red spots	14
e a c b P	Brown, yellow spots	10
E A C B P	Pale sepia, red agouti	15
E A c B p	Pale sepia, yellow agouti	12
E A C b p	Pale brown, red agouti	13
E A c b p	Pale brown, yellow agouti	13
E a C B p	Pale sepia ⎫	
E a c B p	Pale sepia ⎬	29
E a C b p	Pale brown ⎫	
E a c b p	Pale brown ⎬	35
e A C B p	Pale sepia, red agouti, red spots	13
e A c B p	Pale sepia, yellow agouti, yellow spots	8
e A C b p	Pale brown, red agouti, red spots	10
e A c b p	Pale brown, yellow agouti, yellow spots	8
e a C B p	Pale sepia, red spots	15
e a c B p	Pale sepia, yellow spots	11
e a C b p	Pale brown, red spots	4
e a c b p	Pale brown, yellow spots	9
TOTAL		399

Consider, for example the 23rd line on the table. Here is a cross between the pure recessive seacbp (with pink eyes and pale brown coat), and one of the genotypes of the hybrid agouti SEaCbp. seacbp ⅹ SEaCbp → SsEeaaCcbbpp. These offspring (SsEeaaCcbbpp) are pale brown. Some have white spots and some have no such spots. The explanation is that the color derives from the interaction of three pairs of genes, all recessive. One pair, *aa* eliminates agouti; in addition, *bb* changes black to chocolate brown and finally *pp* reduces the intensity from chocolate to pale brown.

As mentioned before, five factors can produce 32 visibly distinct types; and actually the guinea pig has six hair color factors producing a theoretical 64 types (assuming no new mutations).

You can therefore conclude that unless your adult guinea pigs are proven pure beyond any shadow of a doubt, you cannot predict the color of the offspring. Even an albino is not necessarily pure. It can carry some pigment genes. An albino male could possibly carry the genetic formula (genotype) SseeaaccBbPp, and his white spots Ss could "wash out" both B and P. If he was mated to an albino female with the same formula, some offspring might be SSeeaaccBBPP and these, theoretically, would be colored.

You are entitled to be confused. Your question is probably: When every character is recessive, why isn't the animal an albino? The explanation opens another Pandora's box of genetic information. Remember the word in the glossary—Allele? Allele is an alternative form of a gene. Not always simply a long—short, or black—white situation, but sometimes a shade-of-grey situation. This is called multiple alleles and albinism in guinea pigs is the result of such a series of multiple alleles. Albinism is carried on the C factor and is arranged as follows:

C   Intense—Black and Red—Black eyes.

c^k Dark-Dilution—Dark Sepia and Yellow—Black eyes.

c^d Light-Dilution—Medium Sepia and Yellow—Black eyes.

c^r Red-eyed Dilution—Dark Sepia and Yellow to White—Dark red eyes.

And finally:

c^a—Albino—Coat white—Eyes pink.

Therefore, we have sseeaaccbbpp as a white-spotted, pale brown, pink-eyed individual—not albino. For an albino, we must establish a whole new strain with the albino factor present. A pure albino with no colors hidden in its genetic makeup might be shown as sseeaac^{a}c^{a}bbpp. It is also possible to have an albino with some genetically hidden color—SsEeaac^{a}c^{a}BBPP.

It took Professor Wright 399 guinea pigs to come up with one table—and the establishing of the pure recessive strain took years. Suffice it to say, the genetic material for infinite variety is available for any serious fancier; for the rest of us, every litter can be like a wheelbarrow full of surprises.

CHAPTER V

VARIETIES

Ignoring the freaks like four rear toes, we have available the genetic material for colors of hair and eyes, for patterns of hair color, for length of hair and for roughness (whorls) of hair. There is not much size variation. Mature boars weigh 34 to 45 ounces and sows a few ounces less. The hair types have arbitrary names which are lost in history but are still used by fanciers.

The wild type, short, smooth hair is called English. It

There are many different coat and color varieties of guinea pigs; shorthairs like the one shown here are among the most popular. Photo by Brian Seed.

is the most common variety because, genetically, it is dominant over the other two types. The long-hair varies in length, but if it is anything longer than the wild short, it is called Peruvian. The roughness factor is also recessive and when it causes whorls (also called rosettes) of hair all over the body it is called Abyssinian. Many long hairs (Peruvian) also display this trait.

Eye color may be black, brown, dark ruby red or pink. Hair color is nearly independent of eye color but a pink-eyed black is probably impossible to achieve because of certain linkages in genes on the chromosome.

Hair color pattern begins with the wild agouti color and runs to solid colors—black, brown, sepia, chocolate, tan, yellow, and white. These are called "self" colors. Also, the agouti is available as a "silver" as well as the wild brownish type. Then we have two and three color possibilities and all occur. For example agouti and white, or tortoise shell, or spotted yellow, or spotted white are all possible to achieve. A belted pattern with a ring of color around the midsection is called Dutch marked.

Add hair roughness, hair length and eye color and have fun; but regardless of what you accomplish you haven't changed the species, or the possibility to breed back to the original black-eyed agouti-colored short hair.

There are genetic charts available in technical texts which list the known mutations which can be established as "varieties" or "strains" through application of genetic principles mentioned in the genetics chapter of this book; but starters would do well to choose an established color pattern and then improve on it. For example, if you like tortoise shell, you might try through selective breeding to produce uniformly marked individuals where each spot is the same size.

If you wish to specialize in albinos, either English or Abyssinian or Peruvian, you may discover that you have a strain which is not pure white albino, but rather Himalayan. This Himalayan variety of albino has some latent color in its genetic pattern, and if such an individual is kept in a cool cage, the hair on its feet, ears, and nose will darken—pale grey or light brown. This is much like the Siamese cat coloring—pale body and dark extremities.

Most breeders will charge more for light self colors than agouti or dark self colors. They also get more money for long hairs than short hairs and also more for rough (rosettes) than for smooth hair patterns. You will discover, as they do, that this is a matter of supply and demand. Long-hairs, for example, are less prolific and more desired as pets.

Varieties are collectors' items, whereas the ordinary pet shop trade will generally settle for less than perfect show stock. This is not to say that pet dealers handle poor quality cavies. No pet dealer in his right mind would buy or sell a sick, weak, deformed, or overage or underage pet. Pet dealers generally offer only sound healthy stock if they plan to remain in business; but few of them have sources of supply which provide genetically pure animals which could win prizes in real competition. If this is what you want to do, you must look for other serious fanciers to obtain your breeders.

CHAPTER VI

CARE

You need not be a surgeon or a barber or a dentist to help your cavy remain healthy and attractive. The effort is minimal, but often very important.

Begin with the 14 toenails. Check them on any new animal you obtain and on your older animals every month or so. The nails do grow and since caged pets rarely have a chance to dig much, the normal wear process doesn't happen. An oversize nail clipper, available in your pet shop or pharmacy, works just fine. Hold the guinea pig or have someone else hold him for you so you can get some strong light to shine through the nails. See where the blood extends to, and cut leaving a little margin for error to avoid damaging the living tissue when you clip the nail. The angle of clipping should approximate the normal angle of wear. Don't cut square across the line of growth, but rather bevel so that the finished cut shows more nail on top and less on the bottom. This new shortened, but still sharp, toenail is what the cavy wants in order to scratch his itch, and scrape around the shavings or hay in his cage.

The next item is hair grooming. You will need nothing for the English short hair; but Abyssinian and Peruvian deserve a little attention now and then with a toothbrush or equivalent. No hair spray or oils, but just brush out the tangles before they get too bad. A lot of hay in the cage tends to help the grooming naturally, but if you keep show-type long hairs, you will want maximum hair length and the cages will probably be furnished with wood shavings rather than hay to avoid wearing down the ends of the longer hairs. When a good long hair is viewed from above, it should be difficult to determine which is the head end, so any wear should be avoided.

There is virtually no hair shedding with cavies, so you must help them conserve what they have, but if impossible tangles do develop, they should be cut out with scissors. Hair balls may be split and peeled open to conserve as much hair as possible, then combed out with the toothbrush.

A bath is rarely necessary. Many cavies go their full eights years without a bath. If you must bathe a new acquisition, use warm water—say 100° Fahrenheit—and rinse the soap out thoroughly. Dry the animal in a turkish towel and be sure to protect it from drafts or chilling for at least 24 hours.

Cavies are most sensitive to chills and drafts. Be sure that their cages are provided with deep tunnel-like nest boxes. A nest box six inches high, six or seven inches wide and twelve inches long is a good start. Smaller boxes will be occupied by younger animals and larger boxes by family groups. They like to crowd in their nest boxes, but also need plenty of perching and scampering room elsewhere in the cage. This aspect of cavy care was also mentioned in the chapter about cages, and is mentioned again here for added emphasis. It is very important.

Back to hair care, you should not trim whiskers since they connect to sense organs which help the cavy to determine what he can squeeze into. Generally speaking, if the whiskers fit, the rest of the pig fits. Most hair care problems stem from crowded cages or lack of bedding or wet bedding. When it comes to adding more cavies to a cage, don't make a pig of yourself!

Teeth should be examined when you get a new animal and then every month or so thereafter. Your cavy will not bite you unless provoked and it is not difficult to hold him up and gently push back the lips to expose the four long front chisel teeth. They should wear uniformly from chewing. If they don't, furnish him with a clean dry beef bone or cuttlebone (obtainable in pet shop bird departments) or dry corn on the cob, or even a stick of wood, maple or oak preferred.

If gnawing doesn't result in even uniform tooth length, you may need to clip the overlength teeth. Don't read this passage and then run out to your cages and start practicing dentistry. Look at your pet's teeth. Watch it eat. Compare it with other cavies. Offer it something to gnaw on and then if you are certain that the front teeth are so long or misshapen that gnawing will never correct the error, you should trim the teeth. Look at a normal mouth before proceeding and then, using a pair of diagonal pliers (electricians clip and strip wire with them), snip off only enough tooth material to permit the cavy to use his front teeth properly for cutting food. Two rules: (1) If in doubt, don't cut. (2) If confused or fearful of doing it wrong— take him to a local veterinarian. His fee will be modest and his technique more assured.

Diseases of cavies are generally simple to diagnose and simple to cure. Practical common sense will prevent most and control the rest.

Hereditary diseases—freaks, misshapen animals—if they are in pain, destroy them—chloroform or have your veterinarian do this. If they are not in pain, just don't use them for breeding purposes.

Wet behinds—Damp cages and too much lettuce and not enough pellets or hay. Also a symptom of a cold. Your pet got damp and chilled. Provide dry bedding and a draft-free cage.

Continual whistling—possibly hungry or lonely.

Sniffles and runny eyes—this is probably the result of a cold. Treat as mentioned before. Also treat eyes with a sulfa drug ophthalmic ointment—available from a pharmacy without a prescription in most states.

Diarrhea—This is serious but rare. Isolate the animal, sterilize his cage and furnish only clean fresh food.

The author examines the toenails of a full-grown short-hair. Unless they are especially long or twisted, they need no clipping.

Don't withhold water. He may need more to make up his loss. Feed more hay or pellets, but no lettuce.

Minor injuries—as a result perhaps of boars fighting. Isolate the patient and rub on a small dab of antiseptic ointment, so-called "first aid cream" found in most home medicine cabinets.

Boils and cysts are rare. See your veterinarian.

Tumors—have your pet humanely destroyed as per hereditary diseases.

Overpopulation—This is sometimes a big problem for pet keepers, mostly their own fault. Pet shops will buy a few and neighbors may take some, but the best control is by keeping boars and sows apart if you don't want offspring. You can't have it both ways.

CHAPTER VII

FEEDING

Cavies know what they like and what they don't like to eat. They simply don't eat what they don't like. Among things they don't like are onions, hot peppers, and possibly some kinds of cabbage. Among the things they do like are apples, carrots, lettuce, timothy hay, clover, potato peelings and ordinary green garden grass. Young animals will nibble on fresh bread or graham crackers soaked in fresh cow's milk. They also drink clean water

Good nutrition is absolutely essential to the good health of your guinea pigs; fortunately, feeding guinea pigs a good diet is not a difficult task, because the commercial cavy foods easily available at pet shops have been specifically designed with the nutritional requirements of the animals in mind. Photo by Harry V. Lacey.

and possibly enjoy an occasional lick of ordinary table salt. Long hairs lacking salt may take to eating each other's hair.

The hay can be as it comes from the field, or in pellet form. Rabbit pellets are great—just be sure they are not moldy. When you feed the pellets, do it from a non-tipping container which will not get damp and which they will not soil. Your cavy will find a spot in the cage for depositing his droppings—just make sure it is not his food tray or his watering can. Ask your pet dealer and he may suggest a bottle and drip tube arrangement for water. Some people provide the same dishes used in rabbit hutches.

If your pet enjoys a special food—say carrots, carrot tops, potato peeling, celery, or even citrus fruits, by all means let him have it. A cavy will not eat a food which is unhealthy.

In one day, one adult cavy will eat the equivalent of one carrot, two stalks of celery, one leaf of lettuce, spinach or chicory, one small handful of hay, one lick of salt and one to 20 sips of water. A nursing mother might demand a little more, and an old boar a little less. (Mrs. Roberts suggests that one reason a cavy is called a pig is because of his tremendous appetite.)

In winter, the pregnant mother and the newborn young might sometimes be offered a drop or two of irradiated cold liver oil in their milk sop. If they are willing to eat it, it probably won't hurt.

Cavies are generally considered to be leaf eaters rather than grain eaters. This is not absolutely true since they avidly eat the seedy tops of hay. They will often enjoy gnawing on a dry ear of corn or a fresh one; and of course there is the bread or cracker and milk used for the milksop. If you plan to feed mostly pellets or dry hay, you must supplement this diet with fresh greens and extra water.

Even with a cage full of hay, this youngster can be tempted out of his nestbox with a crunchy stalk of chicory.

There seems to be no way to keep cavies in top condition without fresh food.

Pet keepers are sometimes surprised their cavies drink "so much." Chances are that these animals are fed mostly dry hay or pellets. Other pet keepers are sometimes surprised in the converse. Investigation generally establishes that those latter cavies are sustained on lettuce, celery and fresh garden grass. It is your job to provide clean water and your pet will determine the quantity. Although cavies seem to eat a lot, you need not limit their food; actually they eat no more than they need and you should bear in mind that there is little more nutrient value in a bale of hay than there is in ten pounds of grain or a can of high protein dog food.

During the summer months, cavies will eat mowed grass, dandelion greens, chickweed, plantain, milk thistle, hogweed, and many other lawn weeds. The home gardener can supply his guinea pig with cauliflower leaves —a big favorite, kale—some varieties of which will grow during winter, Brussels sprout stalks, escarole, cabbage and savoy, and chicory—easy to grow and prolific until late fall.

When using grocers' greens, wash thoroughly to remove insecticides that may be present and harmful to the cavies.

Roots, including carrots, beets, swedes, kohlrabi and turnips, keep for days and sometimes weeks and make excellent food when there are no greens available.

A nutritious mash should be a part of every cavy's diet. This can be made up from bran, ground oats, maize or barley meal. The grains can be dampened with water or milk. Add linseed occasionally, for coat improvement and general conditioning of the pet. Since grains are fattening, limit the quantity to about three teaspoonfuls a week. Discard that which is not eaten immediately, for it spoils rapidly.

The can-within-a-can in an all-glass aquarium, used as a cage. This 24-inch by 12-inch tank is large enough for two youngsters, or just this old boar.

CHAPTER VIII.

DIET AND NUTRITION

The digestive system of the cavy is not efficient. Cellulose is broken down by bacteria in the intestine to release digestible material. These intestinal bacteria (sometimes called flora) are vital for the survival of the guinea pig and anything which kills them will kill the cavy, too. Aureomycin cannot be administered for this reason, and most of the other wonder drugs will also do more harm than good.

Another point to remember about guinea pigs' diet is

that they cannot generate vitamin C but they do need it. Lack of vitamin C causes scurvy and the control is, of course, green food and even fresh citrus fruits if they will eat them. The author knows of several instances where guinea pigs ate a small ration of fresh orange in their diet and seemed to relish it. Vitamin C is also called ascorbic acid and is available in tablet form, but green foods are easier to feed, and cheaper too. Sprouted grain is also a good source of C.

Milk, especially for nursing sows, is important in diet but you should be sure it is pasteurized since cavies are especially sensitive to tuberculosis. Another problem with milk is that if you feed your pet a diet heavy with biscuit or pellets containing dry milk, and then later feed liquid milk, there is a risk of sudden death. Apparently this is a complicated medical matter of sensitization.

The need for vitamin D is not clearly established, and it may be unnecessary under otherwise normal conditions.

Vitamin E is vital and without it, muscular dystrophy, lack of ability to reproduce, and death result. Fortunately, most hay-vegetable or pellet-vegetable diets provide enough E to satisfy their needs.

Generally, the normal diet of guinea pigs provides sufficient quantities of vitamins and minerals and the only one to watch is "C" if the hay is not supplemented with green vegetables, fresh apple, or possibly citrus fruit.

If large quantities of green food are needed for a colony, your grocer might help with the outer leaves of vegetables. This is fine, so long as care is taken to feed only the fresh, crisp, unwilted parts. The guinea pig has a delicate digestive system and stale food will upset and possibly sicken him.

CHAPTER IX

TAMING AND TRAINING

A cavy is a stupid animal. It survives in nature because it has few natural enemies, is not competitive, has simple needs, and is long-lived. It doesn't survive by its wits, but rather by its shyness.

Its feet can carry it, dig a little, and scratch itches. Old boars kick a little. Food is not held in the feet—as a squirrel does. Travel is limited to flat surfaces or gentle slopes. There is no gliding or jumping or climbing. It is just a clean cuddly hairy lump that whistles.

If your pet is especially shy and you wish it were more affectionate, there are several things you might try. None is guaranteed to work. (Remember that even some people are institutionalized all their lives because they don't respond to other life around them.) But with patience and some intelligent kindness on your part, your guinea pig has a good chance to succeed at learning a few things.

Start with the cage. Be sure it is large enough to permit the animal free movement. The cage should be something a cavy can call "home." Incidentally, a small cardboard carton for a nest box should have no bottom, since your cavy will probably soil it and the accumulation of moisture will cause odors, to say the least. Let the droppings fall in dry hay or wood chips and the moisture will quickly evaporate, leaving the cage sweet and clean. This bottomless nest box is sometimes the clue to taming a cavy. Give him one. *Lure* him out of it with food—something special, like carrot or apple or lettuce. If *this* works, make him push past your finger to get to the food in the palm of your hand. If *that* works, make him reach and pull or, better still, sit on your palm to eat the food. Remember, food is the lure.

Another approach is by filling a cage with loose hay, a source of water and one cavy. He will hide in the hay, but being hungry, he will eat it and eventually eat away his hiding places. If he is not frightened by people or dogs during this period, he will hardly realize that he is safe and happy in the unprotected cage. Don't expect a five minute miracle, but rather a two or three-week campaign directed toward the theme that you are his friend and the cage is his safe home.

If your pet whistles, he is probably well on his way to being tamed. This means that he will come to the cage door or to you when he hears or sees you, and that he will climb into your hand for a tidbit. Don't expect much more. The picture of the cavy standing up and begging for lettuce is much more than you should normally expect.

Baby cavies *should* be handled after their first week. This will help keep them from being shy of humans as they grow up. Hold them in your lap, or some other way to assure that they will not fall if they run off. Petting, whistling, offers of fresh food, all these help to keep your pet gentle and friendly. This is about all you should expect.

If you get an old shy specimen, you can still try all the methods mentioned here and the chances are good that you will reach your goal, but it might take a little longer.

Remember that you are starting out with a shy, stupid animal—don't push, and don't expect instant miracles.

CHAPTER X

SHOWING CAVIES

The British are great at this—showing guinea pigs. A prize boar will be put out at stud for a good fee. Backyard breeders are active throughout the British Isles; they attend shows, join clubs and call their hobby a "fancy." In the U.S.A., pigs is pigs, and a pet show with a big cavy section is a welcome surprise.

Standards for any show are simple and straightforward. The animals must be healthy, bold, robust, active, and clean. The ears should resemble rose petals, soft, small, rounded, drooping. The face should be short; eyes bright and prominent; the nose blunt and Roman. The body should be "cobby." Cobby is an English word, and it suggests an animal which is stocky and short legged. Webster says "round or plump."

Colors should be clear and crisp—not muddy or faded. The tortoise and white is difficult to obtain. It should have small same-size patches of white, black and red uniformly all over. "Self" is a solid color, and rather easy to establish through breeding. Dutch is the ringed pattern common in rabbits and other domestic animals. Three-color Dutch are especially desirable.

For the show, hair may be short—English, long— Peruvian, or whorly (rosetted)—Abyssinian. A long hair should have really long hair, *et cetera*. Avoid mixing the breeds. This will get you nowhere. If you live in the U.S.A. and really want to become deeply involved in cavy breeding and showing, the first thing you should do is plan to move to the British Isles.

Those Americans interested in showing their cavies can contact the American Cavy Breeders Association, R. 1, Box 159, Lockport, Ill. 60441; or the American Rabbit Breeders Association, 2403 Lincoln Ave., Cleveland, Ohio 44134, for information.

An outdoor double-deck cavy hutch, containing three 20-inch nest compartments. Spacers may be placed in the screened enclosure.

CHAPTER XI.

COMMERCIAL ASPECTS

It is not easy to get rich raising cavies. Don't try. Chances are that you will barely break even should you *try* to make money. If, however, you just keep them for fun and sell the surplus to local pet dealers or possibly to a nearby college, you can probably cover all your expenses except labor.

The difference is a subtle one, but then in most businesses the difference between a profit and a loss is really not very much—just a few per cent oftentimes. One more litter per year per sow is what will keep you from becoming a full-time professional, but if you can get over that hump, you could probably do as well or better selling shoes or pruning trees or delivering milk.

One important aspect of cavy culture is that the animals need so little care. For example, 20 or 30 dairy cows will keep one farmer busy; but one cavy culturist can gather food, choose breeding stock, clean cages and generally oversee a herd of several thousand. Now, 2,000 cavies might represent 1,500 mature brood sows, and each sow might be responsible for 50 young per year. You have to figure out how to get rid of 75,000 cavies a year for an average of $1.00 each. If you can sell them. Big if.

With $75,000 per year gross, and expenses of heat, light, rent, food, amortization of the cost of over 1,000 cages, and miscellaneous costs like advertising and delivery, there *might* be $20,000 left for taxes, telephone, insurance, and if there is anything left after that, salaries. Remember that cavies are like us. They eat seven days a weeks. Someone must water and feed them daily—even if *you* want to go on vacation. So assume no epidemic disease, no big bills for inoculations, and a customer always waiting for your production. Then hooray! Your profit after all expenses might be $1,000 on an investment of building and equipment of over $10,000. Now, 10 per cent is not much profit on a risky venture, when you remember that between 1969 and '72 "Triple A" Blue Chip First Mortgage Utility Bonds paid an average of about 8 per cent, and no cages to clean.

So then, who does breed guinea pigs? Back yard and basement breeders on a part-time evening and weekend basis . . . Pet dealers who can't find a good reliable source of supply . . . Retirees and senior citizens who can always fall back on their Social Security, pensions and Medicare if the pig business goes to pot . . . Laboratories and schools who need special strains, colors, sizes, or one sex, or some other odd requirement . . . Hobbyists who produce more than they care to keep for themselves. Somehow the supply and demand have evened out—so don't plan to make a really big splash.

One way to show a good but small profit is to specialize in only the most desirable colors and patterns of Peruvians and then sell them mail-order through magazine classified advertising. It takes nearly as much effort to produce a one dollar short hair agouti as a six or seven dollar really stylish Peruvian. Remember your production will drop to about one-half of the figures given previously if you breed fancy long hairs. They seem to be less prolific on the long haul. Peruvians are not for the mass market.

If you plan to try mail-order, check first with local shipping companies for packaging instructions. Ship "Express Charges Not Prepaid."

Watering jar is simply a pie-pan-like base with a standard Mason jar filled with water and turned upsidedown on it. Standard gravity-feed water bottles are available at pet shops and are safer and more hygienic than homemade devices.

Another way to make a little money is to schedule your breeders to produce what a laboratory or medical school needs at a particular time. This takes some sales effort, missionary work and planning with the customer but sometimes it will pay off.

Still another way to make money is to find a large pet shop or a chain of pet shops and contract for schedule production at pre-set prices.

The flesh, except in communities with strong Latin-American culture, is valueless; don't go after this market unless you live where the people already eat them. There is nothing worthwhile in the skin, fur, or hair; and if you develop a strain with tails, the chances are good that they will go blind.

The problem of an assured supply of quality cavies for a mass market and a pet shop was solved in Groton, Conn. by Mr. Richard Smith, proprietor of an attractive, well-stocked pet shop there. Mr. Smith breeds most of his small mammals in large modern buildings at Stone Hill Farms, also in Groton but several miles from his shop. The area is zoned to permit animal breeding; and the buildings were especially designed by Dick Smith for their intended purposes.

Screened hutches line the outer south side of one building, protected by overhanging eaves. These are for rabbits throughout the year, and they may also house cavies in mild weather. Other cages and enclosures, and even whole rooms are set aside for hamsters, gerbils, purebred cats, and of course, cavies.

The cavies are kept in screened cages approximately two feet by four feet. These cages are made from a very heavy gauge rectangular wire mesh, galvanized after weaving. Each cage is furnished with one or two nest boxes measuring 12 by 18 inches and about eight inches high. Also, in each cage, is a galvanized sheetmetal pellet feeder and several watering bottles. Hay and wood shavings are the bedding. The pellets are supplemented by fresh greens fed daily.

One cage might have a dozen or so weaned saleable youngsters, or a few old sows and their babies, or a colony consisting of a boar and a few sows. The cages are inside the building in wintertime, but may be moved into an open, protected shed in late spring, summer and early autumn.

Mr. Smith is thus able to supply his shop with regular stock and even sometimes fill a special request for a certain color such as tortoise shell or silver agouti. He would probably like to produce even more long hairs, but to get really long hair, the animals would need caging to keep them apart, clipping of breeding stock, and of course, there would be fewer offspring for the same effort. So he produces English and Abyssinian, mostly; and he is able to satisfy not only his retail customers but he can even ship some surplus wholesale stock into the nearby Rhode Island pet market.

Dick Smith emphasizes the importance of fresh greens to supplement the pellet and water diet. He is certain that without the fresh food supplement, his animals could never achieve the quality required.

A cat and two cavies get along well in this home, but as a general rule cavies should be protected from all other animals.

CHAPTER XII.

THE CAVY TODAY

During the Herbert Hoover period, mentioned in the beginning of this book, there were three things working for the cavy. Two were books: One entitled "100 Million Guinea Pigs," written when the population of America was about 100 million, was an exposé describing how the public consumes unsafe or untested products. With this book came the concept that when something is tested on any animal, that animal (or man) is a "guinea pig."

Much medical research at that time was in fact performed on cavies. Since then, new techniques make smaller animals more convenient. This has been a trend

This rough-coated albino was trained to stand on his hind legs— a rare feat for a cavy.

in medicine for many years. For example, the former standard test for human pregnancy called for a rabbit. Later, the Aschheim-Zondek test and the Whitney-Burdick test utilized mice, and the rabbit test for human pregnancy was left behind.

As the rabbit is no longer popular, so also is the cavy. Most of his job in the laboratory has been taken over by the mouse and hamster. Color variations in both these small rodents have been fixed through selective breeding and even such traits as susceptibility to certain diseases have been established in some strains of both mice and hamsters. Of course, both of these latter laboratory animals are smaller, eat less and crowd more. One thing they both lack is longevity, and so for long-term tests on the effect of drugs or insecticides, the cavy is still useful. It is much cheaper to maintain than a cat, dog or monkey in the same laboratory, and it will live nearly as long. Longevity, then, was the second thing working for the cavy.

The other book mentioned before was a humorous story by Peter Finley Dunne in a popular collection about the delivery of a pair of cavies which was held up by a railroad freight agent because he wanted to collect the rate for swine. As he put it—"pigs is pigs" and of course while he held up the shipment, it multiplied. This was quite funny and to this day the cavy is credited with great reproductive powers. Actually, for research requiring production, the mouse, hamster or the chicken does better.

So, now it's a new ball game and new rules in effect. Laboratories design more tests for shorter duration and more individuals; therefore the long useful life of the cavy in the laboratory rarely outweighs its larger size and lower reproductive rate. This then, is the cavy . . . less wanted now in the laboratory, but for the same reasons a wonderful housepet . . . Enjoy it!